99 E4

∞MICROWAVE∞
SWEETS&LOLLIES

Quick and easy recipes for your microwave

Isabel Webb

The Five Mile Press

The Five Mile Press Pty Ltd
22 Summit Road
Noble Park Victoria 3174 Australia

First published 1995
Text copyright © Isabel Webb
Designer: Greg Mason
Photographer: Mannix
Editor: Maggie Pinkney
Production: Emma Borghesi

Printed in Singapore by Kyodo Printing Co.

National Library of Australia Cataloguing–in–Publication data

Webb, Isabel.
Microwave sweets and lollies.

ISBN 0 86788 942 X.

1. Candy. 2. Confectionery. 3. Microwave cookery. I. Title.

641.853

CONTENTS

Microwave sweet-making is much easier, faster and less messy than conventional confectionery-making. It eliminates the seemingly endless wait for evaporation involved in making sweets on top of the stove, because less water is used. And there are no burnt pans to clean, due to the more even distribution of heat. Another advantage of making sweets in the microwave is that it gives you greater flexibility to recover from certain situations (see Reheating the Syrup, page 10).

For best results, make the quantities given in these recipes. Don't try increasing them because microwaves aren't designed to cope with large mixtures. Also, some mixtures, e.g. jellies and fudges, rise during cooking, so smaller quantities are easier to control. Be sure to follow the recipes carefully and to read all the information in the following section (Before you Begin) and you'll be delighted with the results. You'll also be surprised at how quick and easy they were to achieve.

Isabel Webb

✑ BEFORE YOU BEGIN ✑

Making confectionery in the microwave is very easy.
However, it is important to read this section carefully
before you start cooking.

Equipment

For best results, plan ahead and have all the utensils you'll need on hand:

- 2–3 litre heat-resistant microwave bowl
- Foil containers
- Slice pan, about 26 cm x 18 cm (10 in. x 7 in.)
- Scales
- Cup and large spoon (for testing)
- Metric measuring cup
- Set of measuring spoons
- Large spoon for stirring
- Spatula or palette knife
- Candy thermometer (not essential but desirable)
- Starch tray (for moulding confectionery)

Basic Ingredients

Sugar: This is of course the basis of all candies. Different types used include granulated, brown or pure icing sugar (for some uncooked candies).

Liquid glucose: This delays or prevents crystallisation and keeps the mixture pliable.

Cream of tartar, lemon juice, vinegar: These help prevent crystallisation and, for best results, must be added if stated in the recipe.

Preparation of Pans

Foil containers: Recycled foil containers of suitable size are handy for setting different sweets. Smooth out any wrinkles, and oil lightly with edible oil.
Slice pan: A small tin or aluminium pan is the most suitable. The surface should be clean and shiny. If not, line with foil, then lightly oil.

Adjusting Cooking Times

All microwaves and power supplies are slightly different, so be aware that cooking times in the following recipes should be regarded as a guide only. These times have been calculated for **650 watt** microwaves, so if your microwave has a higher or lower wattage you'll have to adjust times accordingly. Remember, the higher the wattage, the shorter the cooking time, and vice versa — the difference will only be a matter of a minute or two. For best results, consult the temperature chart opposite.

For Best Results from Your Microwave

Clean and dry the microwave turntable before you start. Any moisture will use up microwave energy and could affect cooking time.

Settings

HIGH	= 100 per cent microwaves
MEDIUM-HIGH	= 75 per cent microwaves
MEDIUM	= 50 per cent microwaves
DEFROST	= 30 per cent microwaves

Temperature Chart

It is important to boil the sugar syrup to the correct temperature so the water evaporates, thus bringing syrup to the right consistency for beating or setting. The following temperatures and/or cold water tests are generally used to determine when the syrup is ready to be removed from the microwave.

Consistency	Temperature	Test
Jelly	110°C (230°F)	Drop a small quantity of syrup into cold water. If it becomes rubbery the mixture is ready.
Soft Ball	112°– 115°C (236°– 240°F)	Drop a small amount into cold water. It's ready if you can easily mould it into a soft ball.
Firm Ball	118°– 120°C (244°– 248°F)	Drop a small amount into cold water. If ready, the syrup should be easy to mould into a ball.
Hard Ball	121°– 130°C (250°– 265°F)	When a small amount is dropped into cold water it should be hard enough to form a ball, and yet still be pliable.
Soft Crack	132°– 143°C (270°– 290°F)	The syrup will be clear. When dropped into cold water it will separate into threads which are hard but not brittle.
Hard Crack	149°– 154°C (300°– 310°F)	The syrup will be golden in colour, and when tested in water it will crackle and snap.
Caramel	170°C (338°F)	The texture should be 'chewy'. The longer the mixture cooks, the darker and harder it becomes.

Syrups that Rise

Non-crystalline types of syrup (these include caramels, toffee, fudges, marshmallow and jellies, Turkish delight and jubes) depend on ingredients such as egg white and gelatine for their texture. Whenever gelatine is included in the recipe it is advisable to use a large bowl as these syrups will rise considerably during cooking time. For the same reason, these syrups can't be reheated.

Avoiding Crystallisation

The single most common pitfall for most home confectionery-makers is crystallisation. This is caused by sugar not being fully dissolved before boiling takes place. If there are any undissolved grains left on the side of the bowl, crystallisation will occur. The following tips will help you to avoid the problem:
- Brush away any sugar from the side of the bowl with a damp pastry brush.
- Place the lid or cover over bowl for one minute after boiling begins, allowing the steam to dissolve any sugar grains.
- Don't stir during or after the boiling process.
- The addition of cream of tartar, vinegar or glucose can help prevent crystallisation. Use only when included in the recipe.

Reheating the Syrup

- If you haven't boiled the mixture to a high enough temperature (and so the syrup is too soft and tacky), you can simply put it back in the bowl and boil it a little longer, until you have the correct consistency. However, if the mixture contains GELATINE it can't be reboiled — it will froth up and boil over.

- Similarly, if a mixture that is to be shaped or used for coating (e.g. barley sugar to be twisted, caramels to be marked or toffee to be used as coating for toffee apples) becomes too cold to work with, you can return it to the microwave for a few seconds, or until it's of a workable consistency.

Moulding Confectionery in Starch

The starch tray is used for moulding fondants, fruit jellies or other confectionery in cornflour. This is what you do:

1   Fill a slice pan, with a depth of about 8 cm (3 in.), with cornflour.
2   Smooth the cornflour with a spatula, then make the required impressions in it with any small object, e.g. a small plastic mould, a cork, a marble or the top of the finger.
3   Pour or pipe the confectionery mixture into each mould, level with the top of the cornflour.
4   When set, pick up each sweet and dust off the cornflour.
5   Store cornflour in a clean dry container for further use. (Always sieve before use to clean and break up any lumps.)

Kids in the Kitchen

Children love making (and eating!) sweets, and will enjoy measuring ingredients and mixing them together. However it is strongly recommended that they are ALWAYS supervised by an adult, and that they should NOT handle hot syrups. These can give bad burns.

Important Points to Remember

- The bowl you use for microwave sweet-making must be sufficiently LARGE (2–3 litre capacity) and HEAT-RESISTANT.
- Just ONE undissolved grain of sugar will cause boiling syrup to crystallise (see Avoiding Crystallisation, page 10).
- All microwave ovens and power supplies are slightly different, so the times quoted are a guide only (see Adjusting Cooking Times, page 8).
- For best results, test the syrup in cold water and/or use a candy thermometer (see Temperature Chart, page 9).
- Candy will continue cooking for a short time after leaving the microwave. The higher the temperature the longer it will cook.
- Foil containers are ideal for setting microwave sweets in, because it's very easy to remove the sweets when they are cold. These containers can be recycled.
- Most mixtures (except those containing gelatine) can be reheated if necessary (see Reheating the Mixture, page 10).
- It is recommended that children are ALWAYS supervised when making sweets.

NOTE:
    * Cochineal - merely red food coloring.

~ FÊTE FAVOURITES ~

Sweets are always top-sellers at any fête or street stall. If sweet-making is a new experience, and your confidence is low, just start with something quick and simple like toffee. I'm sure you'll be pleased with the results.

2 cups sugar

¼ cup water

2 teaspoons vinegar

½ cup hundreds and thousands

1   Place all ingredients into a large heat-resistant microwave bowl.

2   Heat on HIGH for 2–3 minutes or until just before boiling point.

3   Remove from microwave and stir to dissolve sugar fully.

4   Return to microwave and boil on HIGH for 6–7 minutes, or until Hard Crack (see page 9) and when golden-brown in colour.

5   Remove from microwave. Allow bubbles to settle before pouring syrup into small paper patties.

6   Sprinkle with hundreds and thousands.

Note: Children should always be supervised when making microwave toffees.

QUICK TOFFEES

This quick and easy recipe is ideal for making smaller quantities of toffee. You can even make just one toffee, if that's all you require. You simply half-fill a paper patty case with sugar and add one teaspoon of water and 1–2 drops of vinegar or lemon juice. Then you cook on HIGH for about one minute.

½ cup sugar

2 tablespoons water

3–4 drops vinegar or lemon juice

½ cup hundreds and thousands or nuts

1   Mix all ingredients together.

2   Place six paper patty cases onto a dinner plate, and half-fill each patty with sugar mixture.

3   Cook toffees on HIGH until they BEGIN to change colour (about 3–4 minutes). Remove immediately as the toffees will continue cooking for a few moments longer. Top with hundreds and thousands or nuts, etc.

4   Allow to cool.

Note: The amount of mixture in each patty determines the cooking time. So if patties are filled to different levels, you'll have to remove the less full ones first. To do this, simply take the plate out of the microwave, and remove the cooked toffees by gently holding the top edge of the paper patty with both hands. Set to one side and return the remaining toffees to the microwave to continue cooking. Children should always be supervised when making microwave toffees.

⟨⟨ TOFFEE APPLES ⟩⟩

1 quantity basic toffee (see steps 1–4; page 14)

2–3 drops cochineal

6–8 unblemished red apples

1   Make basic toffee, adding the cochineal before heating.

2   Lightly grease apples with margarine or butter and place a wooden skewer or stick into the centre of each apple.

3   Dip apples into hot toffee and place on a greased tray to cool.

2 cups sugar

4 tablespoons liquid glucose

¼ cup water

60 g (2 oz) dark cooking chocolate

2 egg whites

½ teaspoon vanilla essence

125 g (4 oz) almonds, blanched halves

1   Place sugar, glucose and water in a heat-resistant microwave bowl. Heat to boiling point on HIGH (about 2 minutes). Stir to dissolve sugar.

2   Cover bowl, return to microwave and boil for one minute. Remove cover. Make sure all sugar grains on the side of the bowl have dissolved.

3   Continue boiling on HIGH until Soft Crack (see page 9). Remove from microwave. Allow to become half-cold.

4   Break chocolate into pieces and place in a microwave bowl. Melt on HIGH for about one minute. Don't stir or over-heat or the chocolate will thicken. Gently stir melted chocolate into mixture.

5   Beat egg whites until stiff. Still beating, slowly add in cooled syrup. Then stir in almond halves and vanilla.

6   Pour into a lightly-oiled foil container or foil-lined slice pan. When cold, break into pieces. Store in an airtight container.

PEANUT BRITTLE

180 g (6 oz) caster sugar

5 tablespoons liquid glucose

2 tablespoons water

30 g (1 oz) butter

1 cup peanuts

1 level teaspoon bicarbonate of soda

1/2 teaspoon vanilla essence

1   Place sugar, glucose and water in a large heat-resistant microwave bowl. Heat on HIGH to boiling point (about 2 minutes). Stir to dissolve sugar. Stir in butter until melted, and add peanuts.

2   Cover and boil for 2 minutes to dissolve any sugar grains on side of bowl. Remove lid. Continue cooking on HIGH until Soft Crack (see page 9), about 4–5 minutes. Remove from microwave and allow to stand until bubbling ceases.

3   Remove any lumps from teaspoonful of bicarbonate of soda. Stir into peanut mixture, together with vanilla essence, for about 2 minutes. (If the mixture isn't stirred sufficiently the brittle will become sticky and tacky.)

4   Using an oiled palette knife, smooth the hot mixture over a sheet of non-stick paper on a heatproof surface to a thickness of about 5 mm (1/4 in.). Leave for 3–4 minutes to cool to a handling temperature.

5   Turn the mixture over on the paper, and stretch the brittle until the peanuts stand out of the mixture. Leave until cold, then break up into pieces. Store in an airtight container.

MARSHMALLOW WAFERS

1 quantity marshmallow (see snowballs, steps 1–4, page 24)

1 packet plain wafer biscuits

½ cup hundreds and thousands

1　Make marshmallow.

2　Place several wafer biscuits on table or flat surface.

3　Using a large spoon, or piping bag and large nozzle, place a generous amount of marshmallow on each wafer, top with another wafer and press down lightly.

4　Put hundreds and thousands onto a plate, then press edges of marshmallow wafers onto them, to coat. Allow to cool fully and set.

CHOCOLATE CRACKLES

250 g (8 oz) white shortening (Copha)

4 cups Kellogg's Rice Bubbles

1½ cups icing sugar

3 tablespoons cocoa

1 cup coconut

1   Melt shortening in a large heat-resistant microwave bowl on HIGH for 2–3 minutes.

2   Add all other ingredients and mix well together.

3   Place 24 patty-pan papers on an oven tray. Fill each with Rice Bubbles mixture. Set aside until firm.

SNOWBALLS

1 cup water

2 tablespoons gelatine

2 cups sugar

4 tablespoons liquid glucose

2–3 drops cochineal (optional)

½ teaspoon vanilla essence

2–3 cups coconut

1   Soak gelatine in water for 2–3 minutes. Add sugar and glucose. If the glucose is very cold and difficult to remove from jar, heat jar on HIGH in the microwave for 30 seconds.

2   Heat mixture on HIGH for 2–3 minutes, then stir to fully dissolve sugar.

3   Return to microwave, and boil on HIGH for one minute.

4   Pour into a large mixing bowl. Allow to cool and beat until mixture becomes thick and white, then add cochineal, if desired, and vanilla. Continue beating to mix these in.

5   Pour into dampened patty-tins and leave to set.

6   Remove from patty-tins. Toss in coconut.

Note: For chocolate-coated snowballs, break 180g (6oz) cooking chocolate into pieces and place in a microwave bowl. Melt on HIGH for about 2–3 minutes. Don't stir or over-heat because the chocolate will thicken. Dip snowballs in warm chocolate, toss in coconut and set aside to harden.

1 cup peanut butter

1 cup brown sugar

½ cup golden syrup

½ cup honey

1 cup unsalted peanuts

8 cups Kellogg's Cornflakes

1 Into a large heat-resistant microwave bowl place the first four ingredients.

2 Heat on HIGH until mixture is melted and smooth, and the sugar has dissolved (about 2–3 minutes).

3 Remove from microwave, and gently stir in peanuts and Cornflakes. (Try not to crush Cornflakes too much.)

4 Pat mixture into an oiled slice pan. Allow to cool.

5 Cut into squares, and wrap in plastic sheeting or store in an airtight container.

 Muesli Bars

1 cup rolled oats

2 cups Rice Bubbles

1 cup coconut

1 cup honey

½ cup golden syrup

1 cup sultanas

1 tablespoon butter or margarine

1   Place all ingredients into a large heat-resistant microwave bowl.

2   Cook on HIGH for 4–6 minutes, stirring once during cooking time.

3   Press into a lightly-oiled square pan. Cool. Cut into slices.

Note: If you want chocolate muesli bars, just add 90 g (3 oz) cocoa to the mixture.

Coconut Ice

3 cups sugar

½ cup water

½ teaspoon cream of tartar

1 teaspoon vanilla essence

⅔ cup coconut

2–3 drops cochineal

1   Place sugar, water and cream of tartar into a heat-resistant microwave bowl. Cover with lid.

2   Heat to boiling point on HIGH (about one minute). Stir to dissolve sugar.

3   Cover. Return to boiling point on HIGH. Remove lid. Continue boiling on HIGH until syrup reaches 115°C (240°F) or Soft Ball (see page 9), about 3–4 minutes.

4   Add vanilla and coconut. Beat until thick and creamy.

5   Press half the mixture onto an oiled pan or foil container.

6   Add cochineal to remaining mixture and press on top of white layer.

7   Allow to become cold and firm. Cut into squares.

 No-cook Coconut Ice

2 cups icing sugar

250 g (8 oz) coconut

1 teaspoon vanilla essence

1 teaspoon lemon juice

2 egg whites, slightly beaten

125 g (4 oz) white shortening (Copha)

2–3 drops cochineal

1   Place icing sugar, coconut, vanilla essence, lemon juice and egg whites into a bowl and mix together.

2   Melt shortening in a microwave bowl on **HIGH** for 2–3 minutes. Pour melted shortening over dry ingredients and mix together well.

3   Press half the mixture into a shallow pan lined with waxed paper.

4   Add cochineal to the remaining half. Press onto the white portion.

5   Stand and cool. Cut into bite-size pieces.

 HONEY JOYS

60 g (2 oz) butter or margarine

½ cup honey

2 cups Kellogg's Cornflakes

½ cup coconut

1   Heat honey and butter in a heat-resistant microwave on HIGH for one minute, or until butter has melted.

2   Stir in Cornflakes and coconut. Return to microwave. Cook on HIGH for 3 minutes. Stir.

3   Fill paper patty-pans with mixture. Allow to cool.

4   Store in an airtight container.

⟋⟍ HONEYCOMB ⟋⟍

1 cup sugar

4 tablespoons golden syrup

4 tablespoons honey

1 tablespoon water

4 teaspoons bicarbonate of soda

1   Place sugar, golden syrup, honey and water in a large heat-resistant microwave bowl.

2   Heat on HIGH to just under boiling point (about 1–2 minutes). Stir to dissolve sugar. Cover bowl with lid or plastic wrap.

3   Bring to boiling point on HIGH for 2 minutes, then remove lid. This dissolves any sugar grains around the bowl sides.

4   Continue boiling on HIGH to a temperature of 130°C (265°F), or Hard Ball (see page 9), about 4–5 minutes.

5   Remove from microwave and allow to cool for 5 minutes. Then stir bicarbonate of soda in thoroughly until the mixture froths up.

6   Spoon honeycomb onto a lightly-oiled foil container or slice pan. Allow to stand until cold. Break up into pieces and fill small plastic bags, tied at the top. This is always a good seller at fêtes.

1 cup water

2½ tablespoons gelatine

2 cups sugar

2 teaspoons lemon juice

1 teaspoon vanilla essence

pink and green colouring

¾ cup chopped nuts

¾ cup glacé cherries

125 g (4 oz) cooking chocolate

60 g (2 oz) white shortening (Copha)

1   Soak gelatine in water for 2–3 minutes. Heat to boiling point on HIGH (about 2–3 minutes). Stir to dissolve gelatine.

2   Stir sugar into gelatine and water, and heat on HIGH to boiling point. Stir to dissolve sugar. Continue boiling on HIGH for 2 minutes. Cool.

3   Pour mixture into a large bowl. Add lemon juice and vanilla. Beat with electric mixer until mixture becomes thick and white.

4   Divide mixture into two parts. Colour one pink, the other green.

5   Have two greased slice pans ready. Pour the pink mixture into one, and the green into the other.

6   When both colours of marshmallow have set, cut up into rough, chunky pieces and combine. Then toss nuts and cherries through.

7   Line a flat container with lightly-oiled foil. Roughly place marshmallows, nuts and cherries onto foil.

8   Melt chocolate and shortening on HIGH until melted (about 2–3 minutes). Pour over top of marshmallows and lightly mix through.

9   Allow to set. Cut into pieces.

1 cup granulated sugar

1 cup brown sugar

2 tablespoons liquid glucose

½ cup water

1 teaspoon vanilla essence

1 cup coconut

1   Place sugar, glucose and water into a large heat-resistant microwave bowl. Heat to boiling point on HIGH for about 1–1½ minutes. Stir to dissolve sugar fully.

2   Return to microwave, and continue cooking on HIGH to 154°C (310°F) or Hard Crack (see page 9).

3   Add vanilla and coconut. Pour into an oiled pan or foil container.

4   Allow to cool, then mark into squares. When cold break into pieces.

5   Store in an airtight container.

⟶ THE LOLLY JAR ⟶

The confectionery in this section is ideal for storing in an airtight jar. If you have children, grandchildren or young nephews and nieces the lolly jar is a must.

Tears will disappear,
A smile will appear,
When the lolly jar is near.

1 cup water

6 level tablespoons cornflour

1 ½ cups granulated sugar

2–3 teaspoons rose-water or crème de menthe

2–3 drops red or green colouring

1   Blend cornflour with half a cup of water in a small bowl. Set aside.

2   Combine sugar and remaining water in a large heat-resistant microwave bowl. Cook on HIGH for about 4 minutes. Stir to fully dissolve sugar.

3   Add cornflour mixture to the syrup and cook on HIGH for about 8 minutes, stirring once or twice during that time.

4   Add selected colouring and flavour. Stir through.

5   Cook on HIGH for 4 minutes, or until the mixture is the consistency of thick jelly and will not drop from a spoon easily.

6   Have ready a foil dish, or slice pan, which has been brushed lightly with cooking oil and then dusted generously with cornflour. Make sure the sides of the pan are also coated.

7   Pour jelly into prepared pan. Allow to cool.

8   Sift together 3 level tablespoons of both cornflour and icing sugar onto a sheet of non-stick paper. Turn Turkish delight onto it, cut into squares and coat each square with the icing sugar mixture. The foil container corners can be cut down for easier removal.

9   Leave until cold, then toss in the icing sugar mixture again.

10   Leave uncovered for several hours until outer side is crusty.

11   Store in a covered container with remaining icing sugar mixture. This will ensure the Turkish delight keeps dry.

Note: If the Turkish delight hasn't been cooked long enough it will not harden sufficiently to make it manageable.

RUSSIAN CARAMELS

400 g can sweetened condensed milk

1 cup brown sugar

125 g (4 oz) butter

2 tablespoons golden syrup

1 Place all ingredients into a heat-resistant microwave bowl.

2 Heat to boiling point on HIGH (about 2–3 minutes). Stir to fully dissolve sugar.

3 Return to microwave with lid or cover on, bring back to boiling point and boil for one minute. (This allows the steam to dissolve any sugar on side of bowl.) Remove lid.

4 Continue boiling on HIGH until the mixture is 170°C (338°F) or dark brown in colour and it leaves the side of the bowl when stirred (about 10–11 minutes).

5 Pour hot caramel mixture into a shallow oiled pan. Allow to cool slightly for about 5–10 minutes.

6 Mark into squares with the back of a knife. When cold, cut or break through.

HUMBUGS

1/4 cup water
2 cups sugar
2 tablespoons golden syrup
45 g (1 1/2 oz) butter
1/4 teaspoon cream of tartar
1 teaspoon peppermint essence

1   Put all the ingredients, except the peppermint essence, into a heat-resistant microwave bowl. Cover. Bring to boil on HIGH (about one minute). Stir to dissolve sugar fully.

2   Cover with lid and boil on HIGH for one minute. Remove lid. Make sure all grains of sugar on the side of the bowl have dissolved. Continue boiling on HIGH until syrup reaches 143°C (290°F) or Soft Crack (see page 9).

3   Pour mixture onto an oiled marble slab or an oiled oven tray and leave to cool slightly.

4   Add peppermint essence to toffee and mix through with an oiled spatula knife.

5   Oil the hands slightly and fold the sides of the mixture into the centre, pulling until the desired shade is reached.

6   Finally, pull the toffee into an even roll of about 2.5 cm (1 in.) in diameter. Cut into cushions, using oiled scissors. Allow to cool. When cold wrap in plastic wrap or foil. Store in an airtight container.

1 cup water

2 cups sugar

1/2 teaspoon cream of tartar

2 level tablespoons gelatine

colouring

flavouring

1 cup icing sugar

1/4 cup cornflour

1   Soak gelatine in half a cup of water.

2   Place sugar, remaining half cup of water, and cream of tartar into a large heat-resistant microwave bowl.

3   Heat to boiling point on HIGH, stirring to dissolve sugar.

4   Cover bowl, return to microwave. Continue boiling for 2 minutes. Remove cover. Make sure all grains of sugar on side of the bowl have dissolved.

5   Continue boiling until syrup is 115°C (240°F) or Soft Ball (see page 9) on testing, about 7–8 minutes.

6   Heat gelatine mixture on HIGH to boiling point (about one minute) and add colouring and flavouring of your choice. Stir hot gelatine into syrup.

7   Pour into damp moulds or a damp aluminium slice pan, ensuring that jellies aren't more than 2.5 cm (1 in.) thick. Allow to cool thoroughly. Cut into squares or remove from moulds.

8   Combine icing sugar and cornflour. Toss jellies in this mixture.

9   Store in an airtight container

Note: If a clear jelly is preferred, strain hot syrup through muslin before setting in moulds or tin.

 Acid Drops

1 cup sugar

2 tablespoons water

2 teaspoons lemon juice

1 teaspoon tartaric acid or citric acid

2–3 drops red or green colouring

1   Place sugar, water and lemon juice into a heat-resistant microwave bowl.

2   Heat on HIGH to boiling point (about 1½–2 minutes). Stir to dissolve sugar. Then cover with lid or plastic wrap, bring to boiling point on HIGH, and boil for one minute. Remove cover. Make sure all the sugar grains on the side of the bowl have fully dissolved.

3   Continue boiling on HIGH until 132°C (270°F) or Soft Crack (see page 9).

4   Gently stir in the colouring of your choice and tartaric or citric acid.

5   Prepare the starch mould (see page 11). Fill each imprint with toffee. Allow to cool. Remove from moulds, and brush away excessive cornflour. Store in an airtight container.

CREAMY FRUIT BARS

1 quantity no-cook fondant (see page 74)

60 g (2 oz) candied peel

180 g (6 oz) glacé figs

125 g (4 oz) glacé cherries

125 g (4 oz) blanched almonds

2 tablespoons lemon juice

1 Make fondant.

2 Finely chop peel, figs and cherries. Cut almonds into quarters. Mix all together. Add lemon juice.

3 Knead the fruit and nut mixture into fondant until smooth.

4 Press pieces into individual moulds, or press evenly at thickness of about 15 mm (½ in.) thick into a shallow foil-lined pan.

5 Leave for 24 hours to set and dry. Cut into squares and wrap in Cellophane paper.

¹/₂ cup sugar

¹/₄ cup water

¹/₂ cup honey

¹/₄ cup lemon juice

¹/₂ teaspoon citric acid

1   Place sugar and water in a heat-resistant microwave bowl. Heat on HIGH to boiling point. Stir to dissolve sugar fully. Cover with a lid or plastic wrap, and boil on HIGH for 2 minutes. Remove cover. Make sure all the sugar grains on the side of the bowl have fully dissolved.

2   Add remaining ingredients. Do not stir. Continue boiling on HIGH until Soft Crack (see page 9), about 3–4 minutes.

3   Prepare a starch mould (see page 11). Fill each imprint with honey mixture. Allow to set. Store in an airtight container. Honey soothers are ideal for winter sore throats and colds.

VANILLA FUDGE

1 cup sugar

5 tablespoons condensed milk

30 g (1 oz) butter

½ teaspoon vanilla essence

1 tablespoon liquid glucose

1   Place all ingredients into a large heat-resistant bowl. Heat on **HIGH** for 2 minutes. Stir to dissolve sugar.

2   Return to microwave. Continue boiling on **HIGH** until syrup reaches 112°C (234°F) or Soft Ball (see page 9), about 5–6 minutes.

3   Remove from microwave. Cool until base of the bowl feels comfortable on the palm of your hand. Beat mixture with a wooden spoon for 4–5 minutes.

4   Pour fudge into an oiled slice pan or foil container. When cold cut into squares.

Note: This fudge improves if stored uncovered in the refrigerator for at least 24 hours.

FRUIT AND NUT FUDGE

1 quantity vanilla fudge (see page 50)

¼ cup chopped walnuts

½ cup dried fruit mix

1   Make vanilla fudge.

2   Just before beating the fudge, add fruit and nuts.

3   Cool until the base of the bowl feels comfortable on the palm of your hand. Beat mixture with a wooden spoon for 4–5 minutes.

4   Pour fudge into an oiled slice pan or foil container. When cold cut into squares.

Note: Fruit and nut fudge improves if stored uncovered in the refrigerator for at least 24 hours.

BUTTERSCOTCH

2 cups sugar

¼ cup water

¼ tablespoon cream of tartar

3 tablespoons softened butter

1   Place sugar, water and cream of tartar into a heat-resistant microwave bowl. Cover.

2   Heat on HIGH to just under boiling point (about one minute). Stir to dissolve sugar fully.

3   Cover bowl. Cook on HIGH until boiling point. Remove lid. Continue boiling until syrup reaches 132°C (270°F) or Soft Crack (see page 9). The toffee should be a light amber colour.

4   Lightly stir in butter until absorbed.

5   Pour into an oiled slice pan or foil container. When partly set, mark into squares.

6   When cold and set, break into pieces and store in an airtight container.

Note: Butterscotch can be gently spooned into a prepared starch tray.

3 cups sugar

1 cup water

1 lemon

½ teaspoon cream of tartar

1   Place sugar and water in a heat-resistant microwave bowl. Heat to boiling point on HIGH. Stir to dissolve sugar.

2   Peel zest from lemon. Place into syrup with cream of tartar.

3   Cook to 115°C (240°F) or Soft Ball (see page 9).

4   Remove lemon zest and add strained lemon juice. Cook on HIGH to 154°C (310°F), or Hard Crack (see page 9). The syrup should be a delicate straw colour.

5   Pour onto well-buttered slice pan, and when candy begins to set (about 5–10 minutes) cut into finger-like lengths.

6   When cool enough to handle, twist each strip. When cold, store in an airtight container.

❧THE CHOCOLATE BOX❧

*Almost everyone finds chocolate irresistible — and it's perfect served
with coffee after a meal. The delicious recipes in this chapter aren't too
difficult, and are ideal for small gifts.*

To Melt Cooking Chocolate

Many of the recipes in this section include cooking chocolate. This is how to melt it in the microwave:

1   Break up chocolate (unless using buttons) and put into a heat-resistant microwave bowl or jug.

2   Heat on HIGH until chocolate is soft and glossy on top.

3   Stir until melted. (As a rule, 125g (4 oz) of cooking chocolate heated on HIGH takes about 4 minutes, but the size and shape of the bowl used can affect the cooking time so it's advisable to check the chocolate each minute.)

Note: If the chocolate hasn't quite melted you can put it back in the microwave, but only for a few seconds. If the chocolate has been over-heated and has become grainy, quickly beat in 2.5 ml (½ teaspoon) of white shortening (Copha) per 125g (4 oz) of chocolate.

MOULDED CHOCOLATE

Fill clean chocolate moulds with melted chocolate, using a teaspoon. Gently tap the mould on the bench to eliminate any air bubbles in the bottom of mould and to ensure a smooth base. Allow to set in the refrigerator for 10–15 minutes. Gently tap out when you want to remove them.

Colour variations: For variations in colour, add oil-based food colourings to white cooking chocolate. Partially fill moulds with one colour and allow to set before adding the next colour.

2 cups sugar

½ cup milk

1½ tablespoons butter

2 tablespoons cocoa

¼ teaspoon cream of tartar

1 teaspoon vanilla

1   Place sugar, milk, butter, cocoa, cream of tartar and vanilla into a large heat-resistant microwave bowl. Heat on HIGH for one minute. Stir to dissolve sugar.

2   Return syrup to microwave and continue boiling on HIGH to 112°C (236°F) or Soft Ball (see page 9), about 5–6 minutes.

3   Remove from microwave. Cool until the base of the bowl feels comfortable on the palm of your hand. Beat with a wooden spoon for 4–5 minutes.

4   Pour fudge into an oiled slice pan or foil container. When cold, cut into squares.

Note: This fudge improves if stored uncovered in the fridge for at least 24 hours.

CHOCOLATE NOUGAT

2 cups sugar

1 teaspoon liquid glucose

1/2 cup water

60g (2 oz) butter

90g (3 oz) dark cooking chocolate

1 teaspoon almond essence

3/4 cup chopped glacé cherries

3/4 cup blanched chopped almonds

icing sugar (for dusting tray)

1   Place sugar, glucose, water and butter into a heat-resistant microwave bowl. Heat on HIGH to just under boiling point. Stir to dissolve sugar.

2   Cover bowl with lid or plastic wrap and allow syrup to boil for 2 minutes on HIGH. Remove cover. Make sure that all the sugar grains on the side of the bowl have dissolved fully. Continue boiling until syrup reaches 115°C (240°F) or Soft Ball (see page 9). Allow to cool for 5 minutes.

3   Break chocolate into pieces and place in heat-resistant microwave bowl. Melt on HIGH (about 3–4 minutes). Beat into cooled syrup with almond essence until mixture becomes thick.

4   Allow to stand for 30 minutes. Knead until smooth.

5   In a microwave bowl, reheat on HIGH to a pouring consistency (about 1½ minutes). Stir in cherries and almonds.

6   Line a slice pan with rice paper or dust to cover base of pan with icing sugar. Pour in nougat. Cover with another sheet of rice paper or icing sugar. Place a board or tray and a heavy weight on top.

7   Leave to set for 5–6 hours, then turn out and cut into strips.

CHOCOLATE GINGER

180 g (6 oz) crystallised ginger

250 g (8 oz) dark cooking chocolate

2 teaspoons white shortening (Copha)

1   Wash excess sugar from ginger pieces. Dry and chill.

2   Break chocolate into pieces. Place into a heat-resistant microwave bowl. Add shortening.

3   Melt chocolate on HIGH for about 4–5 minutes, or until mixture is smooth and runny. Care must be taken, because if the chocolate is over-heated it may thicken, making it unusable.

4   Dip chilled ginger pieces into chocolate. Drain and cool.

CHOCOLATE DATES

250 g (8 oz) dates

125 g (4 oz) cooking chocolate pieces

180 g (6 oz) sugar

2 tablespoons boiling water

½ teaspoon vanilla essence

1   Remove stones from dates through a small lengthwise slit.

2   Place all other ingredients in a heat-resistant microwave bowl. Melt on HIGH (about 3–4 minutes).

3   Fill dates with the chocolate mixture, gently pressing the edges together. Allow to cool and harden.

wow! these are a touch of heaven!

CHOCOLATE ALMOND
AND RAISIN BALLS

¾ cup chopped raisins

¼ cup sweet sherry

125 g (4 oz) cooking chocolate

½ cup chopped almonds

½ cup chocolate splinters or coconut (for coating)

1   Soak raisins in sherry overnight. Next day, stir in almonds.

2   Break chocolate into pieces, and place in a heat-resistant microwave bowl. Melt on HIGH (about 3–4 minutes). Stir in fruit and nuts.

3   Form teaspoonfuls of this mixture into balls. Roll in coconut or chocolate splinters, to coat. Set in refrigerator on a plate or tray to harden.

SCORCHED ALMONDS

250 g (8 oz) dark cooking chocolate

2 teaspoons white shortening (Copha)

180 g (6 oz) blanched almonds

1   Break chocolate into pieces, and place in a heat-resistant microwave bowl. Add shortening.

2   Melt chocolate on HIGH (about 3–4 minutes) or until mixture is smooth and runny. Be careful not to over-heat the chocolate or it may thicken, making it unusable.

3   Stir almonds through chocolate, then remove individually. Drain away excess chocolate. Set on a plate or smooth surface until hard.

SCORCHED PEANUTS

250 g (8 oz) dark cooking chocolate

2 teaspoons white shortening (Copha)

180 g (6 oz) unsalted whole peanuts

1   Break chocolate into pieces. Place into heat-resistant microwave bowl. Add white shortening.

2   Melt chocolate on HIGH for about 4–5 minutes, or until mixture is smooth and runny. Be careful not to over-heat the chocolate or it may become too thick, making it unusable.

3   Remove husks and dip peanuts into chocolate. Drain and allow to harden.

125 g (4 oz) cooking chocolate

¼ cup coconut

1   Break chocolate into pieces and place in heat-resistant microwave bowl. Melt on HIGH (about 3–4 minutes). Stir in coconut.

2   Place teaspoonfuls of the mixture onto a dry, shiny tray or smooth sheet of foil.

3   Allow to set in refrigerator for 10–15 minutes.

MOCHA ROUGHS

acquired taste?

250 g (8 oz) cooking chocolate

60 g (2 oz) white shortening (Copha)

2 teaspoons instant coffee

120 g (4 oz) coconut

1   Break chocolate into pieces into a heat-resistant microwave bowl. Add shortening and coffee. Heat on HIGH until melted (about 4–5 minutes). Add coconut and stir gently to blend all ingredients.

2   Place teaspoonfuls of mixture on trays, cover with wax paper and chill until firm.

60 g (2 oz) butter or margarine

1 egg yolk

1 heaped tablespoon cocoa

125 g (4 oz) dark cooking chocolate

1 cup cake crumbs

1 dessertspoon rum or brandy

½ cup chocolate splinters

1   Lightly cream butter or margarine, egg yolk and cocoa together. Melt chocolate in microwave on HIGH for 1–2 minutes and add to creamed mixture. Now add the cake crumbs, rum and brandy.

2   Mix together sufficiently to bind mixture.

3   Form mixture into small balls and roll into chocolate splinters.

4   Set aside to harden in a cool place or refrigerator.

RUM BALLS

180 g (6 oz) icing sugar

125 g (4 oz) softened butter

1 tablespoon rum or rum essence

250 g (8 oz) dark cooking chocolate

¾ cup crushed walnuts (or chocolate splinters)

1   Stir icing sugar into softened butter until smooth. Add rum or essence and mix through.

2   Break chocolate into pieces and place in heat-resistant microwave bowl. Melt on HIGH (about 4–5 minutes). Stir into sugar mixture until blended.

3   Form teaspoonsful into small balls. Roll in crushed walnuts. Place in fridge on a plate or tray until set.

CHRISTMAS BONBONS

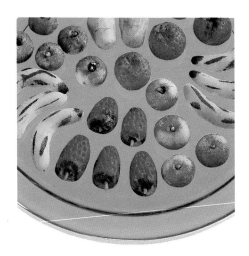

Christmas is the time to forget about the calories and enjoy yourself. What is Christmas without a special bowl of home-made sweets? Attractively boxed and wrapped, sweets also make a festive gift.

250 g (8 oz) white shortening (Copha)

1 cup Rice Bubbles

1 cup powdered milk

1 cup icing sugar

1 cup mixed dried fruit

60 g (2 oz) glacé cherries

1 cup coconut

1   In a heat-resistant microwave bowl melt shortening on HIGH for 2–3 minutes.

2   Mix all other ingredients together, then pour in the melted shortening and mix well together.

3   Press mixture into a slice pan and allow to set firmly before cutting into small finger-like lengths.

COOKED FONDANT

This fondant is used to cover Christmas or wedding cakes. It's also used as the basis for various sweets and chocolates.

2 cups sugar

¼ cup water

1 tablespoon liquid glucose

1 teaspoon lemon juice

1   Place all ingredients into heat-resistant microwave bowl.

2   Heat to boiling point on HIGH. Stir to dissolve sugar.

3   Cover bowl. Return to microwave, and continue boiling for 2 minutes. Remove cover. Make sure all sugar grains on side of bowl have dissolved.

4   Continue boiling until syrup reaches 115°C (240°F), or Soft Ball.

5   Remove from microwave. Allow to cool about 8–10 minutes, then beat with a wooden spoon until mixture is thick and creamy. Knead with the hands until smooth and workable.

No-cook Fondant

2 tablespoons liquid glucose

2 cups icing sugar (plus extra for dusting)

1 egg white

1 teaspoon lemon juice

½ teaspoon vanilla

1   Warm glucose in a cup on **HIGH** for about one minute.

2   Sift icing sugar into a bowl. Make a well in the centre. Add egg white and glucose. With a spoon, mix from centre of icing sugar outwards. When nearly all the sugar is mixed, knead with the hands.

3   Turn onto a board or bench dusted with sifted icing sugar. Knead until smooth and satiny.

4   Knead in lemon juice and vanilla.

¹/₂ quantity fondant (*see page 72*)

1 cup crushed walnuts

1 Place fondant in a heat-resistant microwave bowl and warm through on HIGH for 30 seconds to one minute.

2 Knead walnuts into fondant. Roll into small balls. Then roll these into extra crushed walnuts. Allow to set firmly.

CANDY ALMONDS

½ quantity fondant (see page 72)

2–3 drops cochineal

1 cup blanched almonds

1   Place fondant into a heat-resistant microwave bowl. Heat on HIGH for 1–2 minutes, or until fondant is the consistency of thick cream. Colour with cochineal.

2   Individually dip each almond into the fondant to coat. Drain. Allow to cool and set.

3   For a thicker coating, dip almonds into fondant a second time.

DEVILLED ALMONDS

60 g (2 oz) butter

125 g (4 oz) almonds

4 teaspoons salt

½ teaspoon cayenne pepper

1   Place butter into a heat-resistant microwave bowl. Heat on HIGH to melt — about one minute.

2   Add almonds to butter and cook on HIGH until golden-brown (about 2–3 minutes).

3   Combine salt and cayenne pepper on a sheet of paper, and shake the hot almonds well until thoroughly coated.

 CHERRY ROLL

1 quantity no-cook fondant (see page 74)

chopped glacé cherries

toasted coconut

1   Make the no-cook fondant.

2   Roll the fondant into a sausage shape, about 7 cm (2 ½ in.) wide, then cover with chopped cherries. Roll into long thin rolls.

3   Roll in toasted coconut, and wrap in waxed paper. Chill until firm.

4   Cut into slices, crosswise.

*To toast coconut: Place about ¾ cup coconut onto a microwave-proof plate. Add 2–3 drops of cooking oil. Stir to mix. Then heat on **HIGH** for one minute. Toss coconut about with a spoon or fork. Repeat this until coconut is toasted.*

Marzipan fruits make a lovely Christmas gift if
arranged in a decorative box.

1 cup icing sugar

125 g (4 oz) ground almonds

1 egg yolk

1 tablespoon orange juice or sherry

1   Sift icing sugar. Add all other ingredients. Mix to a firm paste.

2   Allow to set for half an hour. Knead until smooth.

3   Divide mixture into three (or more) portions and form into differently-shaped fruits. Here are some suggestions:

Apples: Roll some of the paste into small balls. Press the stem portion of a clove into the top of each, and colour lightly with red or green food colouring, using a fine paint brush.

Bananas: Shape part of the mixture into small crescents, and brush lightly with yellow colouring. Add a touch of melted chocolate or brown food colouring to each end and some portions of the side.

Strawberries: Shape a small portion of the mixture to represent a strawberry. Prick here and there with a skewer, lightly colour red. Press small green leaves (cut out of marzipan) into top.

2 cups sugar

¹/₄ cup milk

1 teaspoon liquid glucose

2–3 drops yellow colouring

¹/₃ cup chopped glacé ginger

1   Place sugar, milk and glucose into a heat-resistant microwave bowl. Heat on HIGH to boiling point (about 2 minutes). Stir to dissolve sugar.

2   Cover bowl, return to microwave and boil for one minute. Remove cover, and make sure all sugar grains on side of the bowl have dissolved.

3   Continue boiling on HIGH until mixture reaches 115°C (240°F), or until Soft Ball (see page 9). Remove from microwave and allow to cool slightly for about 5–6 minutes.

4   Beat until mixture begins to thicken. Then fold in yellow colouring and ginger.

5   Press mixture into an oiled foil container or slice pan.

6   When set, cut into squares.

APRICOT BONBONS

1 cup icing sugar

60 g (2 oz) coconut

1 egg white

1 teaspoon lemon juice

6–8 glacé apricots

1 cup extra coconut

1   Combine icing sugar and coconut. Mix to a paste with lemon juice and stiffly-beaten egg white. Allow to stand 1½ –2 hours to dry slightly.

2   Cut apricots into chunky pieces. Flatten out a dessertspoonful of the icing mixture and wrap around an apricot chunk.

3   Roll in extra coconut and then mould into a ball. Set aside to dry. Continue this process until all the icing mixture has been used.

GINGER FUDGE

1 cup sugar

2 tablespoons milk

60 g (2 oz) butter

1 tablespoon liquid glucose

1/4 cup finely-chopped crystallised ginger

1   Place all ingredients into a large heat-resistant microwave bowl. Heat on HIGH for 2 minutes. Stir to dissolve sugar.

2   Return to microwave. Continue boiling on HIGH to 112°C (236 °F) or Soft Ball (see page 9), about 5–6 minutes.

3   Remove from microwave. Cool until the base of the bowl feels comfortable on the palm of your hand. Beat mixture with a wooden spoon for 4–5 minutes.

4   Pour fudge into an oiled slice pan or foil container. When cold cut into squares.

Note: Ginger fudge will improve if stored uncovered in the refrigerator for at least 24 hours.

No-cook Cherry Fudge

60 g (2 oz) cream cheese

2½ cups icing sugar

½ cup coconut

½ teaspoon vanilla essence

60 g (2 oz) chopped glacé cherries

60 g (2 oz) dark chocolate

1   Beat cream cheese until soft. Gradually mix in the icing sugar, coconut, vanilla and cherries.

2   Press into a greased square pan. Chill.

3   Break chocolate into microwave bowl. Heat on HIGH to melt (about 1–2 minutes). Spread over the top of chilled cherry fudge.

4   Mark into squares, chill, and cut.

‿❧ INDEX ❧‿